Magic City

Also by Yusef Komunyakaa
Dedications & Other Darkhorses (1977)
Lost in the Bonewheel Factory (1979)
Copacetic (1984)
I Apologize for the Eyes in My Head (1986)
Toys in a Field (1986)
Dien Cai Dau (1988)
February in Sydney (1989)
Neon Vernacular (1993)

Magic City

Yusef Komunyakaa

Wesleyan University Press

Published by University Press of New England

Hanover and London

Wesleyan University Press

Published by University Press of New England,

Hanover, NH 03755

Printed in the United States of America 5 4 3 2

CIP data appear at the end of the book

Acknowledgments appear on page 59.

Contents

Magic City

Venus's-flytraps

I am five,
   Wading out into deep
     Sunny grass,
Unmindful of snakes
    & yellowjackets, out
      To the yellow flowers
Quivering in sluggish heat.
   Don't mess with me
      'Cause I have my Lone Ranger
Six-shooter. I can hurt
   You with questions
     Like silver bullets.
The tall flowers in my dreams are
   Big as the First State Bank,
     & they eat all the people
Except the ones I love.
   They have women's names,
     With mouths like where
Babies come from. I am five.
   I'll dance for you
     If you close your eyes. No
Peeping through your fingers.
   I don't supposed to be
     This close to the tracks.
One afternoon I saw
   What a train did to a cow.
     Sometimes I stand so close
I can see the eyes
   Of men hiding in boxcars.
     Sometimes they wave
& holler for me to get back. I laugh
   When trains make the dogs
     Howl. Their ears hurt.
I also know bees
   Can't live without flowers.
     I wonder why Daddy

Calls Mama honey.
All the bees in the world
Live in little white houses
Except the ones in these flowers.
All sticky & sweet inside.
I wonder what death tastes like.
Sometimes I toss the butterflies
Back into the air.
I wish I knew why
The music in my head
Makes me scared.
But I know things
I don't supposed to know.
I could start walking
& never stop.
These yellow flowers
Go on forever.
Almost to Detroit.
Almost to the sea.
My mama says I'm a mistake.
That I made her a bad girl.
My playhouse is underneath
Our house, & I hear people
Telling each other secrets.

The Whistle

The seven o'clock whistle
Made the morning air fulvous
With a metallic syncopation,
A key to a door in the sky—opening
& closing flesh. The melody
Men & women built lives around,
Sonorous as the queen bee's fat
Hum drawing workers from flowers,
Back to the colonized heart.
A titanous puff of steam rose
From the dragon trapped below
Iron, bricks, & wood.
The whole black machine
Shuddered: blue jays & redbirds
Wove light through leaves
& something dead under the foundation
Brought worms to life.
Men capped their thermoses,
Switched off Loretta Lynn,
& slid from trucks & cars.
The rip saws throttled
& swung out over logs
On conveyer belts.
Daddy lifted the tongs
To his right shoulder . . . a winch
Uncoiled the steel cable
From its oily scrotum;
He waved to the winchman
& iron teeth bit into pine.
Yellow forklifts darted
With lumber to boxcars
Marked for distant cities.
At noon, Daddy would walk
Across the field of goldenrod
& mustard weed, the pollen
Bright & sullen on his overalls.
He'd eat on our screened-in

Back porch—red beans & rice
With ham hocks & cornbread.
Lemonade & peach Jello.

The one o'clock bleat
Burned sweat & salt into afternoon
& the wheels within wheels
Unlocked again, pulling rough boards
Into the plane's pneumatic grip.
Wild geese moved like a wedge
Between sky & sagebrush,
As Daddy pulled the cable
To the edge of the millpond
& sleepwalked cypress logs.
The day turned on its axle
& pyramids of russet sawdust
Formed under corrugated
Blowpipes fifty feet high.
The five o'clock whistle
Bellowed like a bull, controlling
Clocks on kitchen walls;
Women dabbed loud perfume
Behind their ears & set tables
Covered with flowered oilcloth.

2

When my father was kicked by the foreman,
He booted him back,
& his dreams slouched into an aftershock
Of dark women whispering
To each other. Like petals of a black rose
In one of Busby Berkeley's
Oscillating dances in a broken room. Shadows,
Runagates & Marys.
The steel-gray evening was a canvas
Zigzagged with questions
Curling up from smokestacks, as dusky birds
Brushed blues into a montage
Traced back to *L'Amistad* & the psychosis
Behind *Birth of a Nation*.
With eyes against glass & ears to diaphanous doors,
I heard a cornered prayer.

Car lights rubbed against our windows,
Ravenous as snow wolves.
A brick fell into the livingroom like a black body,
& a riot of drunk curses
Left the gladioli & zinnias
Maimed. Double dares
Took root in night soil.
The whistle boiled
Gutbucket underneath silence
& burned with wrath.
But by then Daddy was with Uncle James
Outside The Crossroad,
Their calloused fingers caressing the .38
On the seat of the pickup;
Maybe it was the pine-scented moonglow
That made him look so young
& faceless, wearing his mother's powder blue
Sunday dress & veiled hat.

Playthings

I

I swung a switchman's lantern
Against dusk. One moment, a dull
Green; the next, somewhere
Between molybdate orange &
Bloodred. My Mason jar of lightning bugs
Flickered. The Rebel blew twice
Before stopping a mile away
At the depot, as silver coaches
Snaked like a whip of hot light.
I was never alone when the conductor
Yelled *Next stop, the Crescent City.*
Mama Mary was there to repeat
The lowdown: "It's ungodly.
Your Aunt Tim was sitting
In the depot one day & a joker
Strutted up to her & said,
'Lady, you're real lucky
With that five-dollar gold piece
Round your neck, 'cause I done
Left my dutch knife at home.'"
My half-dead lantern signaled
To the Dog Star, a screech owl
Hooted my name, Brer Rabbit
Gazed out of his thorny sanctuary,
& then my mother's voice
Was loud as a train whistle.
I flung down the jar,
Weaving through saw grass,
& tried to beat my shadow
Home.

2

Mother taught me how
To snap off skinny, half-
Green reeds & whittle them clean
With penknives & shanks of glass
Till they were light as balsa.

We arranged triangles into
Hexagons. Looping cotton twine,
Mixing flour paste, we rolled out
Yards of pale butcher paper
Over a frame tall as a man.
Once she took off her red slip
& ripped it into a kite tail,
& later I almost couldn't see the boy
Hugging the black transformer
Like a war drum, as helmeted
Linemen worked him down
Off the singing wires.
I watched the big boys
Make their streamlined models
Dogfight over cornfields.
Laced with razorblades,
A dragon's tailspin
Slashed the late afternoon
Sky, as March bullied
Raintrees & a girl
In a crimson dress.

3
Round, woven out of pine
Straw, its dome-shaped lid
Like a Chinese hat.
When Grandmama held it in her big hands
She'd chant *Africa, Africa.*
The raised design smooth
As a scar on an old face.
Sunlight rushed into her bedroom
When she lifted the top.
Rhinestone combs, bracelets,
Rings stealing a secondhand halo,
A wooden token
She called a plug nickel:
Good for One Dance.
I'd turn the Gullah basket around
& around in my hands.
It was good work;
Someone's heart in it.

7

I tried to weave my own
But learned weeks later
The needles had to be green.
It would take fifteen years
For Grandmama to say it was woven
By her Aunt Sarah who lived in Chicago
Forty years, passing.

4

I'd spit
On the sidewalk
& jab the popgun's
Pencil-size plunger—
Whittled from a foot
of mop handle—
Till its tip
Flared soft
As a brush.
The barrel
Was eight inches of bamboo.
Chinaberries
Popped thirty feet
Into the air.
Vacuum & tension,
The sucking sound
Of the plunger
Drew the soul
Back
Into
Itself.

5

You cut a handle from a forked
Branch & peel away the bark,
Rounding & rasping it down to
True balance. You turn it over
In your hands to see if the feel
Is right. Next, you take out
An inner tube of red rubber;
Cut two strips straight as a surgeon,
Biting your bottom lip
& humming as you work.

Birds start to leave the trees
& powerlines. Cats & dogs hide
In their unlit worlds, under houses,
As you eye a stockpile of cast-iron
Shards arranged in a corner of the porch.
Sweat & dirt will polish the handle.
This isn't a store-bought slingshot,
What the boys in The Terrace call
Niggershooters. You have twine
& a stock notched just right.
For an ammo pocket you find a tongue
Inside the pair of keepsake shoes
Hidden in the back of your mother's
Closet, the alligator skin your grandfather tried
To break in before dying.

Yellow Dog Café

In a cerulean ruckus
Of quilts, we played house
Off the big room where
They laughed & slowdragged
Weekends. *The eagle flies*
On Friday. The jukebox pulsed
A rainbow through papery walls.
We were paid a dollar to guard
Each other. I was eight
& S.C. Mae fourteen,
As we experimented with
The devil. Mill workers
Changed money in the briny
Glow of bootleg, overpowered
By the smell of collards, catfish,
& candied yams. Granddaddy Gabriel
Worked the cash register
Beside his second wife, Rosie
Belle. I heard my mother
& father laugh like swimmers
Underwater. A raw odor
Of lilies & sweat filled the room;
My cousin's hands moved over me
Smooth & tough as a blues guitar.
Somebody swore they saw
A silhouette with a gasoline can
The night S.C. Mae ran away
With a woman's husband.
For weeks they sifted ashes
But the gutted studs & braces
Only leaned against the wind,
Weak as a boy & girl entwined
On the floor. That June
Granddaddy drove a busload
Up north: the growers paid him
A dollar a day for each pair of hands.
He wanted to rebuild those nights,
Their circle of blurred cards.

The bus grunted between orchards,
& by late August I had enough
Fire-blackened nickels & dimes
To fill a sock, but only a few pickers
Came back after a season of wine-stained
Greenbacks sewn inside coats
& taped to the soles of their feet.

Happiness

When I'd win the fight
Over whose turn it was,
I sat on the top doorstep,
Grinning out into the Fourth
Of July, turning the freezer
Handle. I rocked to a tune
In my head, satisfied
I could hear Satchmo's horn
On his birthday. "Dippermouth
Blues." Hydrangeas bloomed
Along the sidewalk & fence.
The freezer's wooden tub
Was packed with ice & salt,
Around a shiny cylinder
Filled with custard & peach
Slices. Caught up in the rhythm
Till an ache crawled
My arms. Fortissimo. Fire-
Works. The swim hole dynamited
A few days earlier, & voices
Rushed up now like loud
Hosannas. Hundreds of lanes
Snaked through oaks, wild fruit
& honeysuckle. Baskets overflowed
The bank. Big boys whistled at girls
& swandived from the tallest trees.
Small boys on the plankwalk
Jostled each other, springing up
& down like pogo sticks.
I turned the handle faster,
But the goat in the tree
Remained: Daddy Red forced
Me to stroke the throat
Before his butcher knife
Caught the sunlight.
The cry was a child's.
Silence belonged to gods.
There was no paradise, no

Cakewalk for demons hidden
In grass. Old Lazy Bones
Shook out his limbs & pinwheeled
A dustdevil's foxtrot. The air
Sweetened with the scent of goat
Cooking over a pit,
& as the icecream hardened
The hurt in my arms
Made me happy.

Seasons Between Yes & No

1

We stood so the day slanted
Through our dime-store magnifying glass.
Girls laughed & swayed, caught
On the wild edge of our scent.
A scorpion of sunlight crawled
Each boy's arm, as we took turns
Daring each other to flinch. Not
Knowing what a girl's smile did,
An oath stitched us to God.

2

Ice & wind cut through trees
Quick as Pompeian lava casting lovers
Into the arms of strange gods.
We brought in two robins,
& the heat from our hands made them fly
A few clumsy feet.
But half-drugged, rising out of hypnosis,
They broke their bodies
Against breath-fogged panes.

3

We held back curses,
Torturing each other with an adagio
Of silence. Little Faust
Games of the heart.
Bets. Dares. Sucker bait.
Romantic & obscene,
We held back cries,
Letting the mosquitoes suck
Till they popped like stars of blood through cloth.

Glory

Most were married teenagers
Working knockout shifts daybreak
To sunset six days a week—
Already old men playing ball
In a field between a row of shotgun houses
& the Magazine Lumber Company.
They were all Jackie Robinson
& Willie Mays, a touch of
Josh Gibson & Satchell Paige
In each stance & swing, a promise
Like a hesitation pitch always
At the edge of their lives,
Arms sharp as rifles.
The Sunday afternoon heat
Flared like thin flowered skirts
As children & wives cheered.
The men were like cats
Running backwards to snag
Pop-ups & high-flies off
Fences, stealing each other's glory.
The old deacons & raconteurs
Who umpired made an *Out* or *Safe*
Into a song & dance routine.
Runners hit the dirt
& slid into homeplate,
Cleats catching light,
As they conjured escapes, outfoxing
Double plays. In the few seconds
It took a man to eye a woman
Upon the makeshift bleachers,
A stolen base or homerun
Would help another man
Survive the new week.

April's Anarchy

All five shades of chameleon
Came alive on the cross-hatched
Snakeskin, & a constellation
Of eyes flickered in the thicket
As quail whooped up from sagebrush.
I duck-walked through mossy slag
Where a turtledove's call
Held daylight to the ground.
Vines climbed barbed wire
& leapt blacktop,
Snuck down back alleys,
Disguised with white blossoms,
Just to get a stranglehold
On young Judas trees.
Thorns nicked my left ear.
A hum rushed through leaves
Like something I could risk
Putting my hands on.
What April couldn't fix
Wasn't worth the time:
Egg shell & dried placenta
Light as memory.
Patches of fur, feathers,
& bits of skin. A nest
Of small deaths among anemone.
A canopy edged over, shadowplaying
The struggle underneath
As if it never happened.

The Millpond

They looked like wood ibis
From a distance, & as I got closer
They became knots left for gods
To undo, like bows tied
At the center of weakness.
Shadow to light, mind to flesh,
Swamp orchids quivered under green hats,
Nudged by slate-blue catfish
Headed for some boy's hook
On the other side. The day's
Uncut garments of fallen chances
Stumbled among flowers
That loved only darkness,
As afternoon came through underbrush
Like a string of firecrackers
Tied to a dog's tail.
Gods lived under that mud
When I was young & sublimely
Blind. Each bloom a shudder
Of uneasiness, no sound
Except the whippoorwill.
They conspired to become twilight
& metaphysics, as five-eyed
Fish with milky bones
Flip-flopped in oily grass.

*

We sat there as the moon rose
Up from chemical water,
Phosphorous as an orange lantern.
An old man shifted
His three-pronged gig
Like a New Guinea spear,
So it could fly quicker
Then a frog's tongue or angry word.
He pointed to snapping turtles
Posed on cypress logs,
Armored in stillness,

Slow kings of a dark world.
We knelt among cattails.
The reflection of a smokestack
Cut the black water in half.
A circle of dry leaves
Smouldered on the ground
For mosquitoes. As if
To draw us to them, like decoys
For some greater bounty,
The choir of bullfrogs called,
Singing a cruel happiness.

                *

Sometimes I'd watch them
Scoot back into their tunnels,
Down in a gully where
The pond's overflow drained . . .
Where shrub oak & banyan
Grew around barbed wire
Till April oozed sap
Like a boy beside a girl
Squeezing honeycomb in his fists.
I wondered if time tied
Everything to goldenrod
Reaching out of cow manure for the sun.
What did it have to do
With saw & hammer,
With what my father taught me
About his world? Sometimes
I sat reading *Catcher in the Rye,*
& other times *Spider Man*
& *Captain Marvel.* Always
After a rain crawfish surfaced
To grab the salt meat
Tied to the nylon string,
Never knowing when they left
The water & hit the bottom
Of my tincan. They clung
To desire, like the times
I clutched something dangerous
& couldn't let go.

Immolatus

She had her feet in the trough,
Nosing into the golden corn,
When Daddy did a half spin
& brought down the sledgehammer.
She sank to the mud.
An oak branch bowed
As they tightened the rope
To a creaky song of pulley wheels.
A few leaves left
For the wind to whip down,
They splashed hot water
& shaved her with blades
That weighed less each year.
Snow geese honked overhead
& Sirius balanced on a knifetip.
Wintertime bit into the ropy guts
Falling into a number-3 tub
That emptied out in a gray gush
Like the end of a ditch
Choked with slime & roses.
Something love couldn't make
Walk again. I had a boy's job
Lugging water from the pump
& filling the iron washpot.
I threw pine knots on the blaze.
Soon her naked whiteness
Was a silence to split
Between helpers & owner.
Liver, heart, & head
Flung to a foot tub.
They smiled as she passed
Through their hands. Next day
I tracked blood in a circle
Across dead grass, while fat
Boiled down to lye soap.

Banking Potatoes

Daddy would drop purple-veined vines
Along rows of dark loam
& I'd march behind him
Like a peg-legged soldier,
Pushing down the stick
With a V cut into its tip.

Three weeks before the first frost
I'd follow his horse-drawn plow
That opened up the soil & left
Sweet potatoes sticky with sap,
Like flesh-colored stones along a riverbed
Or diminished souls beside a mass grave.

They lay all day under the sun's
Invisible weight, & by twilight
We'd bury them under pine needles
& then shovel in two feet of dirt.
Nighthawks scalloped the sweaty air,
Their wings spread wide

As plowshares.   But soon the wind
Knocked on doors & windows
Like a frightened stranger,
& by mid-winter we had tunneled
Back into the tomb of straw,
Unable to divide love from hunger.

The Smokehouse

In the hickory scent
Among slabs of pork
Glistening with salt,
I played Indian
In a headdress of redbird feathers
& brass buttons
Off my mother's winter coat.
Smoke wove
A thread of fire through meat, into December
& January. The dead weight
Of the place hung around me,
Strung up with sweetgrass.
The hog had been sectioned,
A map scored into skin;
Opened like love,
From snout to tail,
The goodness
No longer true to each bone.
I was a wizard
In that hazy world,
& knew I could cut
Slivers of meat till my heart
Grew more human & flawed.

The Steel Plate

They said Mister Dan
Came back from World War II
With a steel plate in his head.
Came back hooked
On Morphine & killed
His need with Muscat.
He came back a hero,
To a ramshackle house
Owned by the Rail Company,
Back to women who came & left
After each government check.

I would close my eyes to see
Metal reflect sunlight
Like a preacher's collection plate.
His tomatoes & sweet corn overtook
The backyard. Peach, plum,
& apricot blossoms deadened
Acid fumes of the papermill.
Fishing poles hung on nails from a wall.
Sometimes I could hear him
Singing a half mile away.
Maybe Creole or German.

But one Saturday he
Was pulled like a moon
Pulls water, dragged naked
Into the midnight street,
Dancing. The next morning
A rain of crushed blossoms
Just wasn't enough to cover
The vaporous smell of human
Feces outside his gate.
His impression in the dirt
Heavier than any white line.

I saw where the police
Blackjacked him to the ground.
Those lilies around that steel-

Gray casket would keep me away
From funerals. Mister Dan's
Dark-brown serge suit . . .
The round plate barely
Beneath a skin of powder
& hair glued into place,
Not able to stop or hide
The sun's gleamy, blue search.

Sunday Afternoons

They'd latch the screendoors
& pull venetian blinds,
Telling us not to leave the yard.
But we always got lost
Among mayhaw & crabapple.

Juice spilled from our mouths,
& soon we were drunk & brave
As birds diving through saw vines.
Each nest held three or four
Speckled eggs, blue as rage.

Where did we learn to be unkind,
There in the power of holding each egg
While watching dogs in June
Dust & heat, or when we followed
The hawk's slow, deliberate arc?

In the yard, we heard cries
Fused with gospel on the radio,
Loud as shattered glass
In a Saturday-night argument
About trust & money.

We were born between Oh Yeah
& Goddammit. I knew life
Began where I stood in the dark,
Looking out into the light,
& that sometimes I could see

Everything through nothing.
The backyard trees breathed
Like a man running from himself
As my brothers backed away
From the screendoor. I knew

If I held my right hand above my eyes
Like a gambler's visor, I could see
How their bedroom door halved
The dresser mirror like a moon
Held prisoner in the house.

Looking for Choctaw

We put down our popguns
& cap pistols, & raised our hands
Into the air, hoping he'd step
From winterberry & hollyhock.
We flung ourselves in a circle
At sunset & fell in the dust,
But we couldn't trick him
Out. He'd walk in our footprints
When we were alone in the woods
Fishing or tracking a jackrabbit
Through wild-gray tobacco.
Heat figures waltzed to a killdeer
As we searched hollowed trees.
He remained in his unblinking
Stillness, years after toy guns
became real ones tucked into belts.
When we parked with girlfriends
In our souped-up four-on-the-floor
Beside Mitch Creek & listened
To Fats Domino & The Shirelles
On WWEZ, we dared him to fight,
But he only left his breath
On windshields, as if nothing
Could hold him in this world.
Not even the fleshy hunger
Forged by what pulls
Greenness through a leaf.
Perhaps we betrayed mystery
So we could become shadows
Of dreamers, as fingers untangled
Saw vines & left us lost
To ourselves. Mama Mary
Was baking molasses tea cakes
Or stirring sugar into lemonade,
Deep in thought, when she turned
& I saw his face carved
Into hers.

Fleshing-out the Season

They said he lived in both houses.
That the black woman
Once worked as a maid
For his wife. The women
Sometimes met in town & talked
Like old friends, would hug & kiss
Before parting. They said
The man's father was a big-time
Politician in Jackson, Mississippi,
& owned a cotton gin,
& the Klan didn't dare hassle
Him. The black woman's house
Was a scaled-down replica
Of the other: both yards
A jungle of bougainvillea,
Azalea, & birds of paradise.
They said there's a picture
Of the three at Mardi Gras
Dancing in a circle of flambeaus.
In summer he always ate
Cones of raspberry ice cream,
& carried a fat ledger
From house to house. Alyce
Clover grew over his pathway.
He sent his white son to Vanderbilt,
The black one to Columbia.
He had read Blake aloud to them;
Pointed out Orion & Venus.
They said both women waited
To divide him. One sprinkled him
Over the Gulf of Mexico,
& the other put him under roots
Of pigweed beside the back gate—
Purple, amaranthine petals,
She wore in her hair on Sundays.

Blackberries

They left my hands like a printer's
Or thief's before a police blotter
& pulled me into early morning's
Terrestrial sweetness, so thick
The damp ground was consecrated
Where they fell among a garland of thorns.

Although I could smell old lime-covered
History, at ten I'd still hold out my hands
& berries fell into them. Eating from one
& filling a half gallon with the other,
I ate the mythology & dreamt
Of pies & cobbler, almost

Needful as forgiveness. My bird dog Spot
Eyed blue jays & thrashers. The mud frogs
In rich blackness, hid from daylight.
An hour later, beside City Limits Road
I balanced a gleaming can in each hand,
Limboed between worlds, repeating *one dollar.*

The big blue car made me sweat.
Wintertime crawled out of the windows.
When I leaned closer I saw the boy
& girl my age, in the wide back seat
Smirking, & it was then I remembered my fingers
Burning with thorns among berries too ripe to touch.

Yellowjackets

When the plowblade struck
An old stump hiding under
The soil like a beggar's
Rotten tooth, they swarmed up
& Mister Jackson left the plow
Wedged like a whaler's harpoon.
The horse was midnight
Against dusk, tethered to somebody's
Pocketwatch. He shivered, but not
The way women shook their heads
Before mirrors at the five
& dime—a deeper connection
To the low field's evening star.
He stood there, in tracechains,
Lathered in froth, just
Stopped by a great, goofy
Calmness. He whinnied
Once, & then the whole
Beautiful, blue-black sky
Fell on his back.

Gristmill

Black hands shucked
& shelled corn into a washtub
While a circle of ancient voices
Hummed "Li'l Liza Jane."
Daddy shouldered a hundred-pound sack
To Mister Adam's gristmill.
The place was a moment of
Inertia. A horde of rough shoes
Against a revolving dancefloor.
Navel to navel. Slip-
Socket to ball-
Bearing & cogwheel.
Gears dragged & caught,
& the machine's calibrated
Rhythm kicked in.
An orgasm of golden dust
Clung to the wooden floor,
To the grass & leaves
Outside. A field holler
Travelled out, coming back
With the same sweaty cries
Elvis stole from R & B,
Like a millstone worn
Bright. Smooth, white hands
Halved the meal & husk:
One for you, two for me.

History Lessons

Squinting up at leafy sunlight, I stepped back
& shaded my eyes, but couldn't see what she pointed to.
The courthouse lawn where the lone poplar stood
Was almost flat as a pool table. Twenty-five
Years earlier it had been a stage for half the town:
Cain & poor white trash. A picnic on saint augustine
Grass. No, I couldn't see the piece of blonde rope.
I stepped closer to her, to where we were almost
In each other's arms, & then spotted the flayed
Tassel of wind-whipped hemp knotted around a limb
Like a hank of hair, a weather-whitened bloom
In hungry light. That was where they prodded him
Up into the flatbed of a pickup.

2

We had coffee & chicory with lots of milk,
Hoecakes, bacon, & gooseberry jam. She told me
How a white woman in The Terrace
Said that she shot a man who tried to rape her,
How their car lights crawled sage fields
Midnight to daybreak, how a young black boxer
Was running & punching the air at sunrise,
How they tarred & feathered him & dragged the corpse
Behind a Model T through the Mill Quarters,
How they dumped the prizefighter on his mother's doorstep,
How two days later three boys
Found a white man dead under the trestle
In blackface, the woman's bullet
In his chest, his head on a clump of sedge.

3

When I stepped out on the back porch
The pick-up man from Bogalusa Dry Cleaners
Leaned against his van, with an armload
Of her Sunday dresses, telling her
Emmett Till had begged for it
With his damn wolf whistle.
She was looking at the lye-scoured floor,

White as his face. The hot words
Swarmed out of my mouth like African bees
& my fists were cocked,
Hammers in the air. He popped
The clutch when he turned the corner,
As she pulled me into her arms
& whispered, *Son, you ain't gonna live long.*

Temples of Smoke

Fire shimmied & reached up
From the iron furnace & grabbed
Sawdust from the pitchfork
Before I could make it across
The floor or take a half step
Back, as the boiler room sung
About what trees were before
Men & money. Those nights
Smelled of greenness & sweat
As steam moved through miles
Of winding pipes to turn wheels
That pushed blades & rotated
Man-high saws. It leaped
Like tigers out of a pit,
Singeing the hair on my head,
While Daddy made his rounds
Turning large brass keys
In his night-watchman's clock,
Out among columns of lumber & paths
Where a man & woman might meet.
I daydreamed some freighter
Across a midnight ocean,
Leaving Taipei & headed
For Tripoli. I saw myself fall
Through a tumbling inferno
As if hell was where a boy
Shoveled clouds of sawdust
Into the wide mouth of doubt.

Boys in Dresses

We were The Hottentot Venus
Draped in our mothers' dresses,
Wearing rouge & lipstick,
Pillows tucked under floral
& print cloth, the first day of spring,
As we balanced on high heels.
Women sat in a circle talking
About men; the girls off
Somewhere else, in other houses.
We felt the last kisses
Our mothers would give us
On the mouth. Medusa
Wound around our necks
As we wore out the day's
Cantillations. They gazed at us
& looked into their own eyes
Before the water broke, remembering
How we firstborn boys loved
Them from within, cleaved
Like silver on the backs of mirrors.
Would we grow into merciful
Men, less lead in our gloves?
That afternoon lives in the republic
Of our bones, when we were girlish
Women in a hermetic council
Of milky coffee & teacakes.
Dragonflies nudged window screens.
When we stepped out
Wearing an ecstasy of hues,
Faceless wolf whistles
& catcalls heated the air.
Azaleas buzzed as we went
House to house. Soon we'd be
Responsible for the chambered
Rapture honeycombed in flesh
& would mourn something lost.

It was harder than running
Naked down a double line
Of boys in those patriarchal woods,
Belts singing against our skin.

Nude Tango

While they were out buying Easter hats
With my brothers & sister,
I stole a third chocolate
Rabbit from the refrigerator
& tiptoed between two mirrors
Where the scent of my parents
Guarded the room. I swayed, bobbed,
Swayed, my shirt a white flag
When it landed on a bedpost.
Something I had to get past
In the pit of my belly.
What were my feet trying to do
When a shoe slid under the bed?
I tangoed one naked reflection
Toward another, creating a third,
As he sprung across the years
& pulled me into the woods:
If you say anything,
I'll kill your mama.
A ripped shirt pocket
Flapped like a green tongue.
Thistled grass bloodied my knees.
God was in the sunlight
Toying with the knife.
Milkweed surrounded us,
Spraying puffs of seeds,
& I already knew the word *cock.*
I shoved out a hip,
Threw my arms around
My image, & fell to the floor
To let it pass over
Like an animal travelling
Through our lives
To leave a mythic smell.

Touch

Goalposts were imaginary lines
East & west of a shotgun
House, as we trampled
Four-leaf clovers into rosin.
No clipping, no kidney jabs,
No roughing up the quarterback.
We huddled around the ball
Like a young tyrannosaurus
Lagging behind his brain.
You cut right.
You go left
& then zigzag
Right. I'll go up the middle,
& everybody else block. The snap
Propelled us like a battering ram,
As if the line between boy & girl
Could break easily as a wishbone.
Joined like centaurs, pleasure
To pain, we slapped hips & buttocks.
Names lay on our tongues
Like holy bread, sweet as Abishag,
& when we stood side by side
We were one, a shirtless
Juggernaut. Women & girls
Fanned at half-lit
Windows. Knowing our bodies
As well as Oedipus that season,
We faced ourselves, leaving
Shirts & skin on the grass.
Glazed with sweat & salt,
We butted heads till stars
Loomed over the redbuds.

Sugar

I watched men at Angola,
How every swing of the machete
Swelled the day black with muscles,
Like a wave through canestalks,
Pushed by the eyes of guards
Who cradled pump shotguns like lovers.
They swayed to a Cuban samba or Yoruba
Master drum & wrote confessions in the air
Saying *I been wrong*
But I'll be right someday.
I gazed from Lorenzo's '52 Chevy
Till they were nighthawks,
& days later fell asleep
Listening to Cousin Buddy's
One-horse mill grind out a blues.
We fed stalks into metal jaws
That locked in sweetness
When everything cooled down & crusted over,
Leaving only a few horseflies
To buzz & drive the day beyond
Leadbelly. At the bottom
Of each gallon was a glacier,
A fetish I could buy a kiss with.
I stared at a tree against dusk
Till it was a girl
Standing beside a country road
Shucking cane with her teeth.
She looked up & smiled
& waved. Lost in what hurts,
In what tasted good, could she
Ever learn there's no love
In sugar?

Albino

A field of blond sage
    Stood between us & them,
Where we planned ambushes
    With paperbags of gravel.

Sometimes their dark-skinned father
    Hugged & kissed their mother
Under the chinaberry tree
    In the backyard: an eclipse:

She was like a sheet of onionskin.
    We were sure this was how
White people were born,
    & they could see better than ghosts

At night. Some summer days
    We shot marbles with ballbearings
For hours before the first punch
    & the namecalling

Erupted. But by dusk
    We were back to quick kisses,
Hollering *You're It* & *Home*
    As we played hide & seek.

One morning in October
    Creola stepped from the trees
At the edge of a shortcut, the scent
    Of the season's last wild berries,

& we sank among the leaves
    Caught between green & gold.
She led me to their clubhouse
    Beside the creek, a betrayal

Of the genes. It was different
    From the time I was seven
In the half-empty barrel of hogfeed
    With Rosie Lee, when my mother

Lifted the lid & uncapped April.
  Maybe that escaped convict
Had found Creola & me playing hooky.
  Her eyes were pink

& startled as a rabbit's.
  An odor in the air made its own
Laws, as if the tongue was a latch
  Holding down a grace note.

The silence between birds
  Was heavy as a bell,
& here an insect could conjure
  The great noise of a fugitive heartbeat.

Halloween, the Late Fifties

After ghosts & goblins
Were tricked home early,
Dragging cardboard moons in the dust,
We older boys became demons.

We munched Baby Ruths & Butterfingers
Before unearthing our midnight
Stash of inner-tube slingshots
Beside the opalescent millpond.

They uncoiled like water snakes
In our hands. We were ecstatic
With blue-gray cartons of rotten eggs
Resting like miniature bombs in silos.

For weeks we ransacked garbage dumps
For those perfect missiles to stockpile.
We ran through honeysuckle,
Taking shortcuts to the next roadblock

We'd construct with tree branches
& upturned garbage cans, unaware
Rear-view mirrors reflected our futures
Like bank robbers in parked Fords & Chevys.

Behind Batman & Dick Tracy masks
We were a blur of denim snagged
By berry bushes at the crossroad
Of an owl's soliloquy.

But we could depend
On mothers & sisters
To dapple iodine on cuts,
On love to get us out of trouble.

Men & women in bedrooms
Floated against pale window shades—
Stink bombs made in chemistry class
Exploded & oozed across verandahs.

We threw at our own houses.
We were the night's slow dance,
Free to think even the police
Didn't dare shoot.

Mismatched Shoes

A tiger shark
Swims from the mother stream,
Away from danger
Or hunger, to an unknown
Planet orbiting a dreamer's head.
My grandfather came from Trinidad
Smuggled in like a sack of papaya
On a banana boat, to a preacher's
Bowl of gumbo & jambalaya, to jazz;
The name Brown fitted him like trouble,
A plantation owner's breath
Clouding each filigreed letter.
He wore a boy's shoe
& a girl's shoe, with the taste
Of mango on his lips.
Gone was his true name
& deep song of Shango,
But for years it was whispered
Same as a poor man might touch
A lover's satin glove
From another life.
The island swelled in his throat
& calypso leapt into the air,
Only to be amputated
By the wind's white blade.
Yet, he could coo big, country women
& glide into an improvised
Jitterbug that tripped
Hearts. All-night blackjack
& moonshine in mill towns
Took him early. We had paid
Our death taxes, but my grandmother
Never stopped whispering his name.
I picked up those mismatched shoes
& slipped into his skin. Komunyakaa.
His blues, African fruit on my tongue.

My Father's Love Letters

On Fridays he'd open a can of Jax
After coming home from the mill,
& ask me to write a letter to my mother
Who sent postcards of desert flowers
Taller than men. He would beg,
Promising to never beat her
Again. Somehow I was happy
She had gone, & sometimes wanted
To slip in a reminder, how Mary Lou
Williams' "Polka Dots & Moonbeams"
Never made the swelling go down.
His carpenter's apron always bulged
With old nails, a claw hammer
Looped at his side & extension cords
Coiled around his feet.
Words rolled from under the pressure
Of my ballpoint: Love,
Baby, Honey, Please.
We sat in the quiet brutality
Of voltage meters & pipe threaders,
Lost between sentences . . .
The gleam of a five-pound wedge
On the concrete floor
Pulled a sunset
Through the doorway of his toolshed.
I wondered if she laughed
& held them over a gas burner.
My father could only sign
His name, but he'd look at blueprints
& say how many bricks
Formed each wall. This man,
Who stole roses & hyacinth
For his yard, would stand there
With eyes closed & fists balled,
Laboring over a simple word, almost
Redeemed by what he tried to say.

The Cooling Board

Prophet Johnson's white beard
Made the children run & hide,
& sometimes they chanted Santa
Santa. He'd lean on his cane,
Shake his head & say,
Lord, the devil's busy today.
Nobody dared light a cigarette
When the prophet was about.
He cursed women who wore lipstick
& called them Jezebels,
Caning the men who blasphemed
& played the dozens.
Because he read minds,
Teenagers would stare up
At the sky when he passed.
Over a hundred, his grey eyes
Were from the Old Testament
& the streetcorner his pulpit:
You can two-time satan
But you can't lick the Holy Ghost.
Once he'd been a gambler,
Was trapped in a knife fight
& died on the doctor's table.
Women sang the blues from Fourth Street
To The Bottom, praying in a room
Scented with periwinkle & fuchsia,
Before he sat up on the cooling board
& requested a pigfoot
& a bottle of Colt 45.

Omen

The quart jar of silver dollars
Glowed in the windowless shed.
Daddy shook, pointing
To the blind demon
Guarding his poorbox
Like a ghost under a legendary
Tree where a black cat
Dogged the southern moon.
He stood frozen at the door,
Waiting for the coach whip
To stand on its tail
& whistle for a woman.
My right hand found a 2x4,
But I let it fall back
Against a barrel of hogfeed,
Happy in the swollen glands
Of my thirteenth year.
Daylight crawled across the floor
Where poison ivy looped
Up through a knothole.
Like a candle flame,
The snake's tongue darted
To the vibration
Of fear & breath. Still,
I don't know how or why
My body made one motion
As I popped off its head
& threw it at my father's feet.

Believing in Iron

The hills my brothers & I created
Never balanced, & it took years
To discover how the world worked.
We could look at a tree of blackbirds
& tell you how many were there,
But with the scrap dealer
Our math was always off.
Weeks of lifting & grunting
Never added up to much,
But we couldn't stop
Believing in iron.
Abandoned trucks & cars
Were held to the ground
By thick, nostalgic fingers of vines
Strong as a dozen sharecroppers.
We'd return with our wheelbarrow
Groaning under a new load,
Yet tiger lilies lived better
In their languid, August domain.
Among paper & Coke bottles
Foundry smoke erased sunsets,
& we couldn't believe iron
Left men bent so close to the earth
As if the ore under their breath
Weighed down the gray sky.
Sometimes I dreamt how our hills
Washed into a sea of metal,
How it all became an anchor
For a warship or bomber
Out over trees with blooms
Too red to look at.

Salomé

I had seen her
Before, nearly hidden
Behind those fiery branches
As she dove nude
Into the creek.
This white girl
Who moved with ease
On her side of the world
As if she were the only
Living thing. Her breasts
Rose like swamp orchids
On the water's rhythm
Along an old path—
Suckholes & whirlpools
Reaching down for years.
A hundred yards away
The black baptists
From Tree of Life
& Sweet Beulah
Dunked white-robed boys & girls.
The fishing cork danced
& then disappeared, but I couldn't
Move in my tall greenness.
A water snake crawled
Along the stunted oak
That grew half in water,
Half in earth. I knew
Salomé's brother, Cleanth,
Hung our cat with a boot lace
From a crooked fencepost—
Knew he pulled on the cat's
Hind legs, a smile on his face,
& it wouldn't be long before
He would join her in the creek
& they'd hold each other
Like Siamese twins at the State Fair,
Swimmers trapped under
A tyranny of roots, born
With one heart.

Between Angels & Monsters

Short & baldheaded,
He paced the line of black boys
Flexing their muscles
& pointed to the ones he wanted.
Caged lions & tigers
Stared out of a lush
Green, eyes pulsing
Like lights from a distant city.

When he pointed to me,
I stepped closer to the elephants.
They moved like they had a history of work,
& knew where to place their feet
To not cave-in platforms
Loaded with stakes & tarp
Heavy as Hannibal's rafts
Tailgating on a river.

Soon we were hammering down steel pegs
& tying-off ropes, as they nudged pylons
Into place. A new world
Swelled under the big top.
Outside, a woman in a stars-&-stripes bikini
Beckoned us. Near the aluminum trailers
A hundred colors heated the day
As women & men moved through doors,

A flash of bodies in bold windows.
A girl plucked a Spanish guitar
In the doorway of a tent
Where an armless man showed us
How he poured coffee & smoked
Chesterfields with his toes;
She placed a brush between his teeth
& he began painting a rose inside a bottle.

The baldheaded man was waving.
He gave each of us a free ticket
& a red T-shirt that said
The World's Greatest Circus.

We could hear the animal trainer's
Whip crack & bite into Saturday.
The smell of popcorn & chili dogs
Covered the scent of dung & dust.

A bouquet of flowers burst from a clown's trumpet.
We stood like obsidian panthers
In a corner of the white world.
It was as if our eyes had met
As she stepped off the highwire;
Her right foot hooked through a silver hoop—
Hanging like a limp flag
Over the invisible empire.

Poetics of Paperwood

Before dawn. Before we knew women
We rolled into the woods Could make us cry,
Just before blue jays We'd dance-walk
Went crazy in the amber Any hunk of wood
& jade light of dragonflies. Up to the red truck
I saw deer ease We pushed on each other—
Back into the green Dropped & shoved,
Future before double blades It flew into place.
Chopped the day loose. We ate lunch under
I learned how to bed A flowered vine that looped
Trees so they fell Down like a noose.
Between an owl's nest & Sardines, crackers,
  beehive. An orange Hi-C,
A woodpecker tapped & a moon pie.
Its syllabic drum I raked my fingers
Like my father's finger Through old leaves
Against my heart & hundreds of insects
When I did something Lit the humus.
Wrong. Junior, you Junior, till after sunset
Kept the saw from We pulled the crosscut
Bending in the wood Through the pine like a seesaw
Like a whiplash. Of light across a map
I saw where locusts Of green fungus.
Sang themselves out of We knew work
Translucent shells Was rhythm,
Still clinging to & so was love.
Whitman's Live-Oak.

Slam, Dunk, & Hook

Fast breaks. Lay ups. With Mercury's
Insignia on our sneakers,
We outmaneuvered the footwork
Of bad angels. Nothing but a hot
Swish of strings like silk
Ten feet out. In the roundhouse
Labyrinth our bodies
Created, we could almost
Last forever, poised in midair
Like storybook sea monsters.
A high note hung there
A long second. Off
The rim. We'd corkscrew
Up & dunk balls that exploded
The skullcap of hope & good
Intention. Bug-eyed, lanky,
All hands & feet . . . sprung rhythm.
We were metaphysical when girls
Cheered on the sidelines.
Tangled up in a falling,
Muscles were a bright motor
Double-flashing to the metal hoop
Nailed to our oak.
When Sonny Boy's mama died
He played nonstop all day, so hard
Our backboard splintered.
Glistening with sweat, we jibed
& rolled the ball off our
Fingertips. Trouble
Was there slapping a blackjack
Against an open palm.
Dribble, drive to the inside, feint,
& glide like a sparrow hawk.
Lay ups. Fast breaks.
We had moves we didn't know
We had. Our bodies spun

On swivels of bone & faith,
Through a lyric slipknot
Of joy, & we knew we were
Beautiful & dangerous.

Sex, Magnolias, & Speed

No begging forgiveness
For my good aim,
For how the rock
Balanced in my hand
As I walked the bridge
Between football & home.
Someone mooned Orion
& a condom filled with piss
Burst at my feet.
Could the girls
Strapped into bucket seats
Make those boys into men?
The windshield glared like a helmet
On wheels, as chrome fins
Gutted the night
& circled back.
That spring I'd learned
A pivot, beginning in the guts
Behind the spleen.
The Chevy left skid marks.
The sky lay against sepia
Mill water where nothing lived
Among dead animals & blossoms.
At the end of the bridge
Below the Dairy Queen
Police lights splashed
Over magnolias & oaks,
But I walked straight ahead
Into the biography of light
& dark, even after they took me
Out to the white graveyard
& used their rubber hoses.

Knights of the White Camellia
& Deacons of Defense

They were in a big circle
Beside Mitch Creek, as it murmured
Like a murderer tossing in his sleep
Between a wife & daughter, demure
As Sartre's Respectable Prostitute
On a feathered bed in July.
The sacrament. A gallon
Jug of bootleg passed from hand
To hand. An orgy of nightbirds
Screeched under the guillotined
Moon that hung like a target
Reflected against each robe.
Bibles, icons, & old lies. Names
Dead in their mouths like broken
Treaties. A spired & cupolaed
Dominion for bloodhounds. Apparitions
Tied to the Lily-cross & Curse.

Next day, in the hard light,
In a show of force,
Dark roses outbloomed
Camellias, a radiance
Not borrowed from the gleam
Of gun barrels. Sons
& daughters of sharecroppers
Who made sawmills
& cotton fields hum for generations,
Encircled the slow-footed
Marchers like an ebony shield.
Bullhorns blared, German
Shepherds whined on choke chains,
& swaggering clubs throttled spring.
Resistance startled crepe myrtle
& magnolia, while a clandestine
Perfume diluted the tear gas.

Nocturne

The high-beam light swung
Through cypresses like a hundred
Copper wires hooked to a shadow
Tugging on the future. Boxcars
Clattered past like shutters closing, opening
A part of me into the unfinished
Night. Bloodhounds howled.
It was the blue inside
A stone, a cracker's stare.
I gazed so long at the horizon
I heard Big Joe Turner cry out
You a devil with nylon hose. Somewhere
Broonzy spat into a tin cup
Beside his bed, dying
Like my grandfather had
When my mother was eight.
Something held me up to dusk
When birds flew homeward
With straw & lice.
The train whistle left leaves shuddering
As the last drop of yellow disappeared.
Sixteen, I sat there
With a hard-on, sipping a Coke
& staring into the eyes of an Asian
Woman under a flame tree.

Butterfly-Toed Shoes

We began at The Silver Shadow
Doing the Hully Gully,
Till we were dizzy with the scent
Of perfume on our hands. The jukebox
Blazed a path across the semi-dark
Dancefloor as we moved like swimmers
Against each other. April burned
Into the night, after the teenage club
Was padlocked & the scarred WWII
Vets who chaperoned went home
To wives. Some cars nosed into
Backwood lanes as wine bottles
Passed from hand to hand, girls
In their laps, but we sped off
Toward Dead Man's Curve
On two wheels, headed for The Plantation
Club slouched a half mile
Back into fragrant pines.
Off-duty deputy sheriffs guarded doors,
Protecting crap tables in the back room.
The place smelled of catfish
& rotgut. "Honey Hush"
Pulled us into its pulsebeat,
& somehow I had the prettiest woman
In the room. Her dress whirled
A surge of blue, & my butterfly-toes
Were copacetic & demonic.
Cream-colored leather
& black suede—my lucky shoes—
I could spin on those radiant heels,
No longer in that country town.
She'd loop out till our fingertips
Touched & then was back in my arms;
The hem of her dress snapped
Like a boy's shoeshine rag.
She was a woman who would take her time,
Unlike the girls an hour earlier.
We were hot colors rushing toward

The darkest corner, about to kiss,
When some joker cut in
& pulled her into his arms.
I was still swept onward by the timbre
Of her breath, her body,
As I moved to the jangle of three
Silver dollars my grandfather gave me
Five years earlier. I didn't see
The flash when her husband burst in.
Someone knocked the back door off its hinges,
& for a moment the shuffle of feet
Were on the deck of a Dutch man of War.
I'm still backing away
From the scene, a scintilla
Of love & murder.

Acknowledgments

Grateful acknowledgment is made to the following publications, in which some of these poems originally appeared: *Arts Indiana*: "Sunday Afternoons," "Looking for Choctaw," and "Happiness"; *The Black American Literature Forum*: "Butterfly-Toed Shoes"; *Callaloo*: "The Whistle," "The Millpond," "The Steel Plate," "Albino," "Banking Potatoes," "The Smokehouse," "My Father's Love Letters," "Salomé," "Between Angels & Monsters," and "Slam, Dunk, & Hook"; *The Georgia Review*: "Believing in Iron" and "April's Anarchy"; *The Kenyon Review*: "Playthings," "Yellow Dog Café," "Fleshing-out the Season," "Gristmill," "History Lessons," and "Knights of the White Camellia & Deacons of Defense"; *New England Review*: "Nude Tango," "Sex, Magnolia, & Speed," "Touch," and "The Cooling Board"; *Ploughshares*: "Venus's-flytraps," "Blackberries," "Temples of Smoke," "Halloween, the Late Fifties," "Mismatched Shoes," "Immolatus," and "Seasons Between Yes & No"; *Red Dirt*: "Sugar"; *River Styx*: "Omen" and "Poetics of Paperwood"; *The Southern Review*: "Glory" and "Nocturne"; *Vox*: "Yellowjackets" and "Boys in Dresses."

Acknowledgment is also made to the following anthologies: *Dynamics of Violence*: "History Lessons" and "Knights of the White Camellia & Deacons of Defense," Duke Univerity Press, 1992; *New American Poets of the '90s*: "Venus's-flytraps," "Sunday Afternoons," "Blackberries," "Temples of Smoke," and "My Father's Love Letters," Godine, 1991.

I wish to thank the National Endowment for the Arts for a fellowship that enabled me to complete this book.

UNIVERSITY PRESS OF NEW ENGLAND
publishes books under its own imprint and is the pub-
lisher for Brandeis University Press, Brown University
Press, University of Connecticut, Dartmouth College,
Middlebury College Press, University of New Hamp-
shire, University of Rhode Island, Tufts University,
University of Vermont, and Wesleyan University Press.

ABOUT THE AUTHOR
Yusef Komunyakaa, recipient of the 1994 Pulitzer
Prize for Poetry and the Kingsley-Tufts Poetry Award
for his book *Neon Vernacular*, is professor of English
at Indiana University. His other books include
Copacetic (1984), *I Apologize for the Eyes in My
Head* (1986), winner of the San Francisco Poetry
Center Award, and *Dien Cai Dau* (1988).

Library of Congress Cataloging-in-Publication Data

Komunyakaa, Yusef.
Magic city / Komunyakaa Yusef.
    p.   cm. — (Wesleyan poetry)
ISBN 0-8195-2205-8. — ISBN 0-8195-1208-7 (pbk.)
    I. Title.
PS3561.O455M34   1992
811'.54—dc20   92-53863
♾